Woman Putting on Pearls

Jeffrey Bean

Grateful acknowledgment is made to the editors of the following publications in which many of these poems first appeared, sometimes in different forms and under different titles: *The Antioch Review*: "The Voyeur Comes Home Drunk," "What the Voyeur Would Live On"; *Barn Owl Review*: "Your Kid and Mine"; *Bateau*: "The one you learned to hope for"; *Chiron Review*: "Canoe"; *Cider Press Review*: "Letters"; *Crab Orchard Review*: "Alfred Sisley: *Snow at Louveciennes*"; *decomP*: "Kid, this is school," "Kid, you have hands"; *The Fiddleback*: "Summer Garden"; *FIELD*: "Song of the Good Body (originally untitled)"; *Gargoyle*: "The Dead Arrive"; *Journal of Medical Humanities*: "Sleep"; *Juked*: "I Come from Indiana," "Newborn"; *Memorious*: "Your Hands on This Rail"; *The Missouri Review*: "Kid, I remember 1968," "Kid, these are train tracks," "Kid, this is Iowa," "Kid, this is October," "Kid, this is the first rain"; *National Poetry Review*: "The Voyeur's Days and Nights" (originally untitled); *New York Quarterly*: "You can lead a horse to water"; *Poet Lore*: "The Voyeur Looks at *The Milkmaid*, Jan Vermeer," "The Voyeur Sees Her Leave in the Evening"; *The Raintown Review*: "The Voyeur and the Fireflies"; *RHINO*: "Love brought me down again"; *River Styx*: "The Voyeur in the Storm," "The Voyeur's Blues"; *Salt Hill*: "After Dinner"; *Subtropics*: "The Bread," "Why I Quit Playing Text Twist"; *Swink*: "On TV," "What Geraniums Smell Like"; *Willow Springs*: "The Voyeur's Gratitude," "What the Voyeur Learned," "The Voyeur's Prayers," "You Don't Love the Voyeur."

Printed in the United States of America

ISBN 978-0-9973102-5-2

RED MOUNTAIN PRESS

Santa Fe, New Mexico

www.redmountainpress.us

For Jessica
and for Olivia

Acknowledgments

Some poems have previously appeared in two chapbooks: *Girl Reading a Letter at an Open Window,* winner of the Cowles/Copperdome Poetry Chapbook Award, published by Southeast Missouri State University Press, and *The Voyeur's Litany,* winner of the Anabiosis Press Chapbook Contest, published by Anabiosis Press. "I Come from Indiana" is included in the anthology *New Poetry from the Midwest 2014,* edited by Okla Elliott and Hannah Stephenson (New American Press). "Kid, this is October" and "Kid, this is Iowa" are included in the anthology *New Poetry from the Midwest 2016,* edited by Okla Elliott and Hannah Stephenson (New American Press). "The Voyeur's Blues" appeared in *Free Verse,* an online column on St. Louis Public Radio's Web page (news.stlpublicradio.org).

I am deeply grateful to Jeffrey Skinner and Sarah Gorham for their help in shaping this collection. Without their incredibly insightful feedback this book would not have been possible.

Many thanks to my colleagues at Central Michigan University—especially Robert Fanning, Darrin Doyle, and Matt Roberson—who supported me throughout the writing of this book. Sincere appreciation goes to Central Michigan University for granting a sabbatical during which many of these poems were written.

Thanks, too, to the wonderful team of Susan Gardner and Devon Ross at Red Mountain Press for bringing this book into the world. Thanks, especially, to Susan Gardner for her outstanding editorial work. And big thanks to Sarah Sousa for selecting my manuscript for the Red Mountain Poetry Prize.

And, finally, heartfelt thanks to my friends and family, especially Barbara and John Bean, David Bean and Jini Puma, Carole and Eddie Powell, and, above all, to Jessica and Olivia, for everything.

HER HANDS, THE BREAD

The bread, the salad, simple, oiled.
       The coats on hooks, exhaling winter smoke.
The hand that was mine, the knuckles,
          the table, smooth oak.
      The girl I'd come to meet, the sky behind her hair,
        shook foil.

Her legs crossed at the ankles, the coiling
       evening traffic, forgettable talk.
The oysters, fat men at the bar, laughs
         like question marks of breath.
      The salt on the roads she came down, the choice

she made, the choice she almost made,
      her mouth there, where I could touch it.

What we tasted, smelled, said, the places on my body
      she touched, the places she did not.
I had been lonely, I had been hungry as a rat.
      The glass, the salt, the road, her hands, the bread.

YOUR HANDS ON THIS RAIL

Your hands on this rail
poised like a pianist's

are birds in the slow movies
my father shot with his Super 8,

jays that live now only on film,
hanging forever in the breezes of the '80s,

the dust of those summers
that stuck in my mouth

like the retainer I'd pluck out
to point at girls on the playground,

a disembodied organ, pink as sex, alive
as the moths I cupped in my hands,

the pulses and smudges they left with me,
their ashy vanishings into that pasture

in Iowa, full of cricket fire,
that held my house and the day

in my twenties you lay on my bed,
peeled off your socks, lifted your throat

up to me, the image of your skin
folding in and in me where

it is still coiled, like a reel of film,
waiting to be threaded through light.

Why I Quit Playing Text Twist

I kept missing *her*. Like in *whiner*,
where I also missed *wren* and *whir*.
I couldn't find *womb* in *bowman*. In *gusted*
I uncovered *dust* and *sued*, but not *duets*.
Who wouldn't find *bile, bite,* and *lie*
in *blithe?* It's harder to find
lite and lithe. In snares
I missed *seas.* Every kid has found *girls*
in *grills* by accident, but not me. I only
got *lugs* and *ugly* in *snugly*, made up *gunsly*.
I saw *sewers* but not *seers*, the *hole*
in *behold*. There *she* was in *pusher*,
lurking with the *user*, but I missed *her*
again, and the *pure* there, the *hue*.

to these train tracks, the ties swollen
with summer heat, the ballast rocks glittering
with shattered things, even in the dark.

The graffiti I carved into the grass
has vanished, but the grass insists
on whispering about it. Soon

the train will grind past, hauling
its flammables into the heart
of the city, fences, red lights,

signs that say *danger*,
cages inside cages where
the coal goes in, the hot feelers

of wires stretch out to the house
where she sleeps, fill it with buzzes
and glow. I will walk the tracks

until I pass her backyard, suck
her lights out through her window.
I will fall asleep with a piece of coal

in my fist like a syllable, until morning
when she comes out for the mail
and I open my hand, holding up that

one word, silent, and brought here to burn.

I study the weather map, looking for you
as though green swaths of rain on the radar
were your hair and smell about to wash
over my city, like you could be predicted,
graphed, and I could dress right, or leave town,
before you blew against my coast, breaking
record highs, the white foam of you
pounding me, my sandy body drinking
your salt, like I could stand outside,
open my mouth, catch you on my tongue,
and you'd become my tendons and pigments, cells
and lipids, the grease I leave on pillows,
earpieces of phones, and forever they would say,
remember the storm, and every year every kid
in school would learn to sing your name.

SUMMER GARDEN

It failed: I kept spading the dirt into
the shape of her hair. Nothing grew. That winter
each day I did a spell: I wrote down what she said,
folded the notes into my pocket, went skiing
in the forest so her breath when she came home
smelled like a katabatic wind
blasting pines. We kissed one night
on the couch, the TV preacher
broke down, finally, said something
so powerful and strange
we wouldn't have needed to fall in love,
but we didn't hear it, not fully, and she went on
buying me beautiful shirts, my closet like
a hothouse, flowers so red I can't sleep.

has written a poem thanking the chair and the floor
for buoying her up, keeping her body from crashing
into the basement, and she is going to read it.

A man comes pounding on your door at 3 a.m.,
scared in the wind, pretending to need
the phone. Nothing comes of it. She and you go on

eating popcorn, moving from lit rooms
to dark rooms. No matter how dark it gets
you can still feel shapes, and sometimes

in her sleep she cries out like a hinge.
Nights when she falls asleep first,
you thank the floor, her body, your body,

for keeping you buoyed and warm and apart.

The girl's fingers slide along
the virginal's keys,
pull triads into air.

The man kneads
his cane against his palm.
Her face in the mirror opens—
toward him? Away?
He wishes she were bread
he could hold on his tongue.

The artist has left a place
for you, an empty chair.
The viola da gamba
lies silent on the floor,
wears silence like

a skirt you could unwrap
if you would kneel down
between the couple,
take the soft wood in
your arms. Can you feel
the notes you don't play?

They slide like fingers
along the skin
of the room.

THE VOYEUR'S BLUES

I lie down in shadows in my yard to watch
heat lightning and you in your kitchen,
your husband around for once, and how you want
to talk to him but can't. You both move when

the other moves—to load dishes, change
clothes, stuff wrappers in the trash,
wipe up the juices and flakes of your strained days
together. The storm is just north, and will miss us,

but the wind is cooling fast. You lift up the sash,
stick in a fan. I love it that you don't know
I slip in with that wind, I drift up your shirt to touch
your held-in places, easing the heat there, the slow

acid of anxiousness climbing your throat like a rope.
I hear you with my telescope.

THE VOYEUR'S BLUES

At night you fold your blouses, your hands
          are all I see.
At night you smooth those creases, your hands
          are all I see.
At noon your window's blank with sun—your window
          watches me.

Standing in my study, I see you argue
          with your man.
I lean, tired, in my study, watch you argue
          with that man.
If you've got my lust for leaving, I've got two tickets
          to Japan.

Sometimes I climb my maple tree and watch you
          from the air.
Sometimes I climb my maple tree, look down on you
          midair.
I'll watch you till I look like bark and squirrels
          nest in my hair.

You've got a prickly blackberry bush—it's blooming
          in your yard.
I'll eat those prickly berries one night in the quiet
          of your yard.
When my mouth turns blue, I'll talk to you
          like I'm praying to the Lord.

I think I've read about you in books of
          poems and ghosts.
I think I've read about you in poems about
          books and ghosts.
You haunt your window, then my head—you stick to
          both like frost.

I see you smiling, laughing, on the sidewalk
          on the phone.
I see you laugh and shake your head, talking
          on the phone.

I love whoever's on the line—he makes me
          doubly alone.

It's nine o'clock and raining, but the sun shines
          on the leaves.
It's almost night and raining, but there's sunshine
          on the leaves.
Tonight I'll live inside your skin like rain
          lives in the trees.

Crumbs on your neck
and your bed where, lying on your back,

you ate a slice of birthday cake
last night with your hands. My tiny licks

of frosting from your fingers.
Sips of shower-water

from your belly button
you missed with the towel after your run

before work, your clean blouse draped on a chair.
Sparks where you pull the hairbrush through your hair.

WHAT THE VOYEUR LEARNED

The afternoon I watched you wash your car
with a sponge and hose in your driveway,
I learned how your hands would feel on my arms,
slippery-cool, soapy, and I learned the way

you would hold me in my filth, if I were yours, and clean
away the bugs and dust I'd have gathered, rushing over
hills for whatever you wanted, wherever you needed me,
and I saw how cold and clear it would be, the water

of your attention, turned at last on the worn down
treads of my hands and feet. I learned you've used me
all this time, unlocked me, climbed inside me and driven
until you've drained my tank. But you could fill me,

too, you could restore my body with soap and cloth,
bring your face close, finish me with your breath.

THE VOYEUR LOOKS AT *A WOMAN ASLEEP AT TABLE*,
JAN VERMEER

The warmth of the room, the tilt and dangle
of pearls against the flush on her face, the lace
on her collar, the open door where a dog was erased
(according to the curator's label), the cloth on the table,

its folds of red and orange like flame in the foreground,
the bowl of gold fruit, the milk-colored jug
(full of what?), the clear glass of liquor, half-drunk
and gleaming, and the poise of her sleeping left hand

like it's still awake and working: which of these
makes it into her dream, if she dreams? I'm here
to imagine it, to paint what is inside her
in my head, to feel her wrist against her cheek.

The way, last night, you shut the blinds in your kitchen,
and I shut my eyes to see the things that live there:
your milk, your bowls, your fruit, your hands, your hair,
your face in your dim window, and my reflection.

SONG OF THE GOOD BODY

Dawn-sick rose-sick word-sick worm-round,
The good body knows to float down
To the tire-smoke roads to the chain-sing scene
Of work, work, his darling, his lust and his leaning,
And steep in the green-shock of screens and un-screened
Calls, of all day screen-green call girls.

O but toward home soft clover bristles,
Near sizzles with motion, and what's cordial,
Immortal jiggles below it and through
And through the raw fellow of the good body.

And he comes down the walk, warm,
Down, down the walk, and sings to Emily,
Sings I am the angleworm, I am the dew,

I am the bird-shine, the caw,
The step-aside robin that eats the fellow raw.

I Come from Indiana

I come from Indiana, where the only thing to eat
is clouds. I was born in a snowstorm, the blizzard of '78,
and like snow I come back every year, shaking my hair,
dancing to the slowest music,
full of whole notes.

I come from Indiana,
where the shoulders of the ground
grow hairy with grasses, where anthills swell up
into heat and the smell of tar shimmering over roofs.
I walk out wearing nothing but a huge coat of corn,
I vanish into the horizon but never leave, like a line
of highway traffic, I throw handfuls of myself into air,
the particles of me gather below streetlights like mayflies,
die in the afternoon then gather again,
night after night.

I come from Indiana, where faces grow plump in dreams
like lettuce in soil and good men in towns pour oil
into mowers a few feet from wild deer sniffing the wind,
hidden behind trees.

I come from Indiana, where the stories about me are true:
the day I stole that policeman's horse,
the day I drove my Honda blindfolded into a tornado,
the day I spray-painted *cellar door, cellar door*
over and over on my girlfriend's cellar door until
her father chased me with a burning log
into the woods, where he couldn't find me because
I was making love to his daughter under a bridge
in a thunderstorm.

I come from Indiana, and when I'm there I enter the air
like a teenager diving from a boat, the hard blade of his
torso slicing the lake while his mother, out of earshot,
calls him home.

WHAT GERANIUMS SMELL LIKE

Like birds.
Like my brother leaving for the lake.
Like the smudge of fireworks on driveways.
Like breath trapped in a canteen.

Like the word *breath*.
Like mice.
Like want.
Like a nickel in a fist.

Like my brother leaving for the store.
Like my brother leaving for the war.

Like a handful of washed hair.
Like my mom humming Johnny Cash.
Like a red towel in the wash.
Like a scrape on a thigh.
Like a Service Merchandise.

Like my dad's violin.
Like a cloth that cleans guns.
Like car leather.
Like a war turned low on a radio.
Like parents getting used to you gone.

Like baby I love you.
Like you are the only one.
Like holes in the knees of jeans.
Like what you weren't supposed to see.
Like drops of blood on a hardwood floor.
Like my brother leaving for the war.

Like ice in a glass.
Like beets.
Like leaving.
Like *please*.
Like bees.

C_ANOE_

Each paddle was stained, tough
like part of a grandfather.

The J-stroke motion hung in my back,
at lunch it made my hunger
feel like circles. Only once or twice
all summer the canoe came out
of the crawlspace, smelling of hymnals.

Only once a possum fell down
on my dad when he hoisted the boat
above his head. I saw it:
the fleshy tail like a penis
touched his neck, he screamed,

dads did not scream. I watched
his body, hanging there
a moment, heaving, his navel
staring down that animal's ancient hiss.

His belly hair moved like milfoil
on the brown stomach of the lake.

but you can't punch him in the face,
especially when he speaks in the voice

of your dead mother, his teeth full
of blackberries she picked

and ate in those watery,
gone Julys. You can follow

her needle into the seam
of your shirt, but you won't be

her young hands, won't know
what they hoped for and forgot.

No more than that horse will drink
or you will raise your fist against the plushness

of his face, your fist, which was never good
at crushing. But you can drink in

the horse-shaped clouds and yards
and suck the thread of your shirt

all the way down to your childhood,
where your mother and her needle

are always working. Listen—

the horse in her young voice
is running through the yards of the dead.

THE DEAD ARRIVE

The dead arrive, wearing your old clothes,
wanting to swap faces.

The dead come on like flu season, moisten
the air, change the smells of trees.

The dead man presses his eyes up to yours.
They fit like a plug in a light socket.

The dead woman shakes ice from her hair,
feeds the shards to neighborhood girls.

The dead are in your attic now, ringing
Grandpa's goddamn Christmas bells.

The dead are in the mud, and your shoes
cannot stop touching the mud.

The dead touch each other
in their boxes like matches.

Like matches, the dead
are red-faced and blind.

You warn your children not to play with them,
while you sleep your children play with them.

The dead lie down. The dead stand up.
They breathe like flames into all of your rooms.

On TV

On TV a model flashed
her hands out under the lights,
made her body slippery
as a ruby. What the hell

had I done worth two shits
was what I thought my beer
can would say to me with its
nasally little song if it sang.

Answer: I had watched turkey
buzzards make their arcs
above untold quantities of corn.
My body was an armchair.

My body might roll out toward the banks
of the loud night like a wave, it might
dance like cellophane in traffic, it might flash
green as TVs against windows.

My beer can closed its eye
and sang upside down a new
TV-name for me, a lovely
sound, out under the lights, far.

SLEEP

is the green shade in you
you press up to.

Lay down your book,
this body, thick loaf, your slow work.

The thrumming dank wood
of your chest, moods

like rings expanding there.
A thin one's a dry year,

a fat one's a green year.
The knuckles of your wants rap your

hard surface, words finger your bark.
Faces from your childhood spray like smoke

from your brain's saw.
This is what you saw:

the good table of your bones
hauled down to the lawn,

pulped, spread like seeds
to turn into mud and birds.

You are in the bed's mouth. It will swallow.
You are the bed's bird. Its swallow.

She wills her body to hold still
against the tug and shove of cloth.
The bunched-up tapestry on the table
spills a bowl of fruit turning soft,

shrinking in shadows cast by her dress.
The paper in her hands looks ruined,
her face is mute. The lion heads
carved on the chair, the sash, the curtains—

all push close to read the news.
We know it's bad. The window knows
how light and all of us get used:
her curls, reflected, look like bones.

No floor, no ceiling in this room.
She's young. She's almost gone.

They arrive through the mail slot, smelling of thumbs,
with the charged freshness of produce, or wings
just cut from a living thing.

They are blind in their bushels,
they do not know what makes their bodies light.
They hurtle over oceans and ice.

They move over roads so long
they turn like roads into names.
They cannot see their names,

they do not understand their clothes,
only that they close to the one face they know
then open to a strange face. Then close.

They come warm to tables
like peppered bread, white, black.
Like us, they do not understand

how they nourish—only that
something swallows them like savory food.
They dream of the time they were meaningless wood.

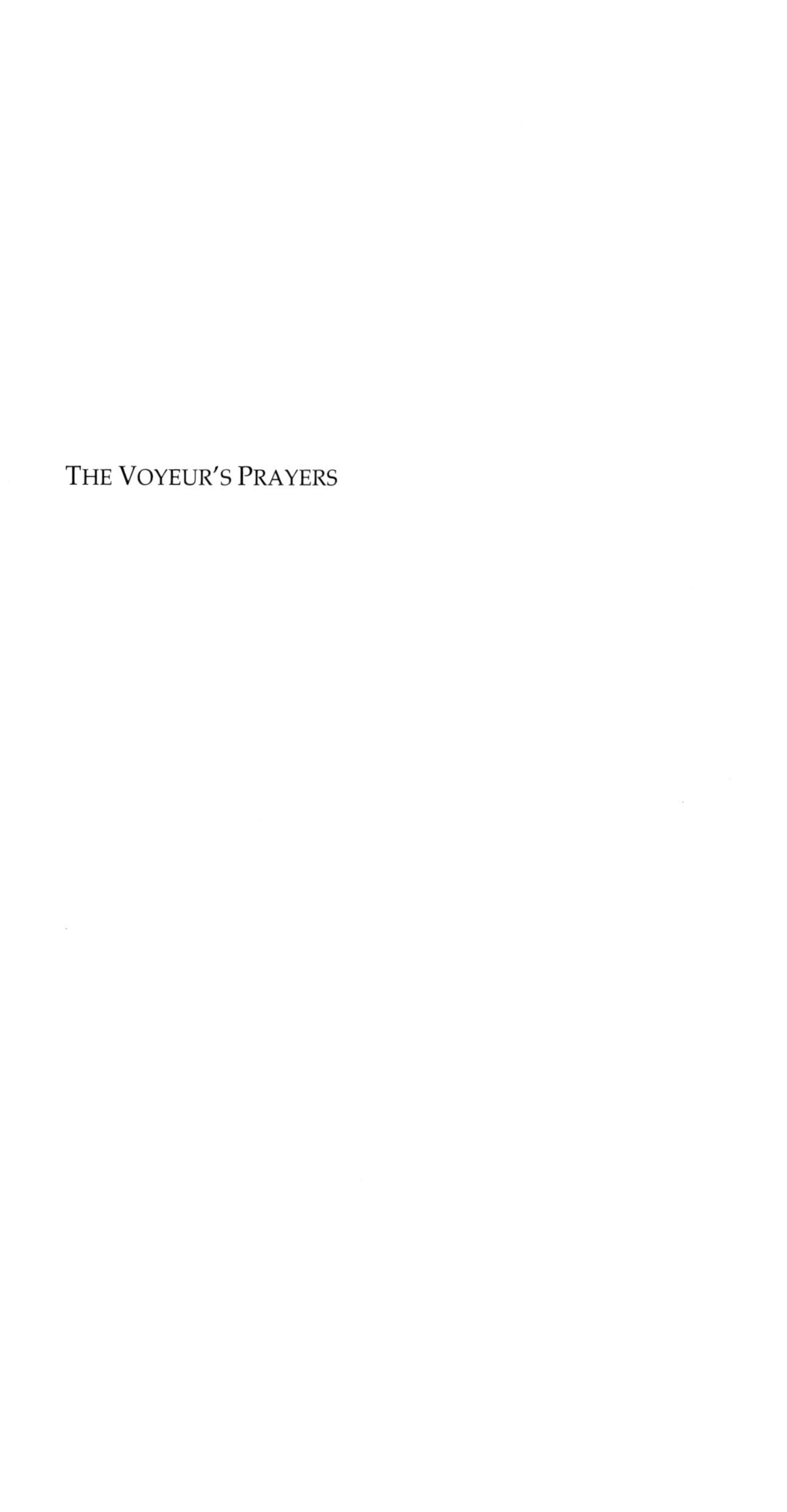

THE VOYEUR'S PRAYERS

I want to taste the air that touches your house.
I want to stand at your door, drunk as unmown grass,

swaying in the wind in your yard, gulping its sweet
green wine. I want to lick the sweat

from your neck, squeeze my tongue
with the yellow tie that holds your hair up

while you run. The water that gushes over your hands—
I want to be that, and slide like your butter-almond

hand soap across the meat of your palms.
Flakes of your skin turn to dust in your rooms

and I want to gather it, stuff it in your closet,
build a cloud and sleep in it, till my dust is your dust.

Climb in your bed. With my eyes, I'll hold your weight.
I'll tap your roof, flash in your mirror. I want to be rain.

When your bedroom light is off I look
at fireflies instead. They spark, spark again,
then fade to black
like someone's mouth or night has swallowed them.
They light to mate, I've heard. Do they choose when,

or is the need to glow unstoppable,
a force so powerful it makes their bodies
climb air and swell
with light so keen, so hot, they're stunned and freeze
in place? The ancient Greeks thought that a sneeze

meant gods were spelling out some prophecy
because you cannot cause it, make it stop,
or even see
what blasts out of you—your eyes screw up,
shut by portentous force. As when your lamp

comes on, you lift your shirt, and I am swallowed
in the bright hole you cut into the night.
I'm not allowed
to un-see you after that. I'm forced to fly here,
eyes screwed shut, abdomen on fire.

Of course, I never follow when you go
to the bar in the middle of our college town
with your friends after work, so I don't know
what you drink—hot-pink cocktails or gin,

straight up. I don't know if the locals
laugh and slap hands, pound shots in little groups,
leaning on pool cues by the neon sparkle
of the jukebox. Do they play metal? Or blues,

the slow kind, John Lee Hooker, over and over?
I don't know if you press against the bar and smoke,
or strut and curl to the thump on the dance floor,
arching your back the way, when you first wake up,

you stretch, reach for the glass on your night table
to cool your throat. I don't know if the bar's floor
is sticky, or covered in spent peanut shells
that crackle as you walk to the back door

with a man, not your husband, your fingers in his collar.
I don't know how you touch him, so I sit,
watch your house, pour tea into a cup, red water
sliding like your tongue in his mouth, and I drink it.

THE VOYEUR LOOKS AT *THE MILKMAID*, JAN VERMEER

Vermeer knows what I watch the days I catch you
in your kitchen: your hands and what they cup
and how they curve to do it. Her sleeves rolled up,
the milkmaid shows us skin sun never gets to.

Vermeer knows that her arms inside her dress
might find our arms, might open, like the bread
beside her, warm as the white cloth on her head.
I hear the trickling milk. I taste a place

inside the jug, the flavor of cold rivers.
I tilt into the light of that Dutch afternoon
and keep on falling till I am the woman,
and I am watching my own parted lips, my fingers.

But I'm not just parts. She's not. Neither of us is there.
In the room without us: bowls, cloths, a closed jar.

The nights you're not there are the nights
I am best at wanting: when I leave my house
without leaving my house, when my face's light
looms as calm as the moon's, my shadow still as moss.

What is it I want to see, watching your empty room,
your empty bed, your empty dresses flung down
on the floor? They remember where you've moved,
describe the shapes of you everywhere you've been,

but not as well as I can. Is it just the wanting
I want? The words I find to wish you would appear
more fervent than any prayer
I've said with my sorry mouth since the beginning?

Now the moon's high, and we both watch your chair.
You are and are not sitting there.

NEWBORN

NEWBORN

My baby is a chubby fire, flaring
all night into the eye of
the video monitor. Birds love her,
call back when she cries them awake
at five a.m. A father

now, I understand birds,
how unbearably thin
their voices are. I will write
in the book of her life
that I swung her up, thumped
with love her plump back,
cleaned and kissed her feet,
played the heavy banjo
of her sobs, stormed through
the upstairs rooms with box fans
all June to cool her down.

I'll never tell her I cried into my eggs
for my old life, or the dream
where she's my thumb grown enormous,
heavy at the end of my arm,
and I have to shred with my one good hand
my endless hair to feed her.

Your Kid and Mine

Your kid climbs trees?
The day my daughter was born
she snuck out the window and *smoked*
a whole oak like a huge cigar. Her breath smelled
weirdly pleasant after that, like sap, rain, and brushfire,
and her first laugh made a grove spring up
plus a lot of bright water and rabbits.

Your kid says the alphabet?
Day two, my daughter knew the constellations.
Her first words were "The cold fishes
of astronomy stretch out above us
while we sleep the dumb sleep of flowers."
That same day, she skillfully arranged a bouquet
of actual flowers, then stole a jeep and won
a regional tae kwon do competition,
all without leaving her bouncy seat.

Your kid plays flute?
My kid *eats* flutes. On day three she cried
Bach's Toccata and Fugue in D minor.
Her mom rushed in
with a violin.

Kid, this is October,

you can make the maples blaze
just by stopping to look,
you can set your clock to the barks
of geese. Somewhere the grandfathers
who own this town lean down to iron
crisp blue shirts, their faces bathing
in steam, and blackbirds
clamor in packs,
make plans behind corn.

You know this,
you were born whistling
at crackling stars, you snap
your fingers and big turtles
slide out of rivers to answer.

You can swim one more time
in the puddle of sun
in your water glass, taste icicles
already in the white crunch
of your lunch apple. Go
to sleep. I'll put on my silver suit
and chase the sky into the moon.

use every part of them to feel
the horsemint. Let's compare
faces—yours is
wonderful/full of wonder
mine is full of wonder
but crushed a little
around the eyes.

This is where we live.
You can smell coffee
through the window screens,
hear living people clinking spoons
if you're up
at the pink hour.

Remember how
at the pioneer village
in Indiana
that huge waterwheel
turned above us, crushed corn
while lookers-on watched
videos about corn facts
on their phone-screens?
How the sunscreen
I spread on your face
smelled like a field
of weeds?

That butterfly agreed,
tasted your eye
with its feet.
In the gift shop, a white horse
eyed you, and you said you knew
it wanted to take you home.

When I dream of horses
I never think
to climb up and ride them.
But you and I will drive
interstates so long

and fast those roads
in our minds will turn
into fat gray horses of light.

And when you grow up, please
remember to keep smelling your hair,
keep loving the crunch
of snow and lettuce.
The coffee-ground smell
of true horses.
Remember to take me
to the last aisle
of the farthest gift shop,
buy me
everything you want.

you learn not to cut up your hand
when you cut out a pink paper bird
the shape of your hand. You learn

to push your face into red Play-Doh
till your face looks up at you from the worktable
and you carry it home. *I* before *E* except

after *C* and vowels and sometimes *Y* your red
face learns to say. Except neighbor and weigh.
When I was in school I walked through snow

uphill with Albert Einstein. Albert
was a worried student. During storms,
he would run beside lightning bolts at just

the right speed and shout SEE? SEE?
I never figured out what he meant. I ran,
though, through my share of thunder. Later,

Arnold Schwarzenegger joined my fifth grade class,
he riddled our chalkboard with Uzi rounds.
I hardly noticed because like always

I was following the action of the clouds
and trees. A lightning bug named Roger lived
in my desk, he needed comforting. I hummed.

In the cafeteria, graham crackers were lifeboats,
skateboards, castle walls. The gravy: the moat.
In gym I sweated and cried my way up ropes

while hairy older kids laughed and threw grapes. I hope
you check in more often than I did, I hope the shapes
in atlases stand up like colorful deer

in your head when someone says *Ecuador,*
Alaska, Pakistan. I know you won't imagine hammers
falling on the spines of your enemies, or hatch plots

to poison villain-versions of your teacher. Instead
you'll tune your recorder impeccably, fall asleep smiling
on a C Major triad, your uncut hands lit up with pastels.

Kid, I remember 1968,

ten years before I was born.
I was a taco. I was eaten

by a beautiful schoolchild
whose hands were like white,

tropical lizards. I must have tasted good—
she lingered on every drop of sauce

and I made her miss her bus.
She stood in the fog and cried

into a scarf until her mother
pulled up on a record player.

You could drive those things
in those days. She was playing

Steppenwolf, spinning through
a red light when the kid got on.

You couldn't stop a record for safety's
sake, especially in the sixties.

You couldn't stop the schoolkid's dreams
of garbage cans full of lightning and butter,

either, couldn't keep her from growing up
and moving out and eating tacos

before naps. She did it
all the time. Woke up with gum

in her hair in a strange room. Her room.
That's where babies come from.

VERMEER: *WOMAN PUTTING ON PEARLS*

Sometimes you get a minute or two,
nobody needs you for once, your body's buoyed
by that grass-and-river feeling after lunch,

you draw back the shutters and the room
takes on the freshness of streams, hard buds
swelling up outside. It's early spring,

you've got your best coat on, ermine trim,
and you lift up a necklace to the light,
to the space and quiet (it's a gift, it asks

to be touched like this), and the places it touches
you, fingertips and throat, become
organs more sensitive than mirrors or eyes.

The V the ribbon makes that holds the pearls
draws the pleasures of the room in closer:
this chair, this table, this blue rug, the tug

of your earrings, your hair bow like a pink, chubby hand,
the downward slope of your forearms, eyelids,
mouth, light all over the wall like words

for what you wanted, words you can't remember
now that you're thinking what the light is *really*:
shattering fire, violent as birth

for billions of years out there in space, that long,
blue-cold cloth, an emptiness from which
sometimes come moons pink as hands in orbit

around a throat, a head, some pearls, warm for now.

The Voyeur's Days and Nights

THE VOYEUR'S DAYS AND NIGHTS

In the middle of the night
you move like a rabbit
in my body's field,
at the edge, out of sight,
you stuff me with litter
and grass, build your nest.

I wake up blind
as a kit, licked clean.

In the morning
you push like roots
through the mud of me,
leave cracks in my crust like texts.

In the afternoon
I am the yard, you are the blade,
you hum above me, cut
until I am bald.

In the day's last red light,
in what I want and forget,
you swing like a spider
then suck out that light,

my trees, my city,
you drink down all my thinking
like a drain.

In the middle of the night
I try your hundred names.

THE VOYEUR VISITS HOME

I went back for awhile to that southern place
of richer weeds, richer corn, crepe myrtles redder
than anything northern, heavy in wet air, wetter
still in spite of drought, the sun's insistent shapes.

Back to the breakfast place where I read and talked
with friends, back to the few friends I still think to call,
their words for things which are my words, their alcohol
my alcohol exactly. Back to greener farms, greener dark

edges of fields, Cooper's hawks and nighthawks hunting
the cool blue patches by the hush of rivers
where I could forget you, go on living without ever
watching the downward curve of your body leaning

to lift up socks, or smooth your calves with lotion,
a place I wouldn't need words. But today I found
you moving in your doorway, a syllable's motion
in a mouth. I tried not to make a sound.

But you need him, and you think you don't need him.
Without him, you're just bones and blood in a shower.
He drinks the light you reflect, enlivens your skin.

Watching, he makes your fragments whole again,
Counts your pulses, stretches out your hours.
But you go on thinking you don't need him.

Those mornings you get up early, go for a swim?
He is that feeling, humming behind white flowers,
Drinking the light, enlivening your skin.

He forgives—no, *savors*—your every slip and sin,
But you don't notice, buried under covers
Fast asleep, thinking you don't need him.

He gives you his fullest thoughts, his richest attention,
He crackles beside you all night, a soothing fire
That drinks the light you reflect, enlivens your skin.

He doesn't want to have and hold you, to *own*
The way your husband does. But he is there,
And you need him, and you think you don't need him.
He *is* the light you reflect. He lives in your skin.

THE VOYEUR COMES HOME DRUNK

I drink my wine, drink it again, and fall
at the feet of your window screen.
The spring air and I find our way in,
trailing your kitchen sounds, the low vowel

of your humming to yourself, chopping greens.
My eyes blurry, I feel tall
for once, lying facedown under stars, my arms full
of your sundress, lifting you close. But I hear that man

you live with, his voice pulls
me back to this wet grass, this fern
I've crushed with my dumb arm. I drink rain
from the bucket under your gutter to cool

my head. Fat moths butt against the panes,
chasing the place where your bare legs flash. Fools.
I am a fool. My ear pressed to dirt, I hear the trickle
of rivers underground. You're drinking from his hands.

THE VOYEUR'S GRATITUDE

This dark afternoon in July, this all-day rain,
means you are home and your lights are on
and I can put down my book and pen
and stand for awhile in my study, in the dark,
and watch you while you work.

You have your work gloves on, your drill,
you're hanging something on your wall,
shelves, or a mirror. You hold three nails
in your pursed lips, stand tip-toe in old jogging shoes
and a paint-flecked tank top, straining. Thank you

for your open curtains, that little mercy,
and for hiring men to trim your trees,
to restore clear air to those places that filled with green
so I can live in them again. Stand with me here a minute,
listen to the rain. We could both go out in it,

we could meet, and talk, try to impress
each other. But we could never be as generous
as your window light. There would be bitterness,
eventually, a closing up. And then ruin, then regret.
I'll go on watching you work, loving the ache of it.

CURLS OF SMOKE

Kɪᴅ, ᴛʜɪs ɪs Iowᴀ,

everything we are is here—
my dead grandmother as a girl
hunting fireflies in tiger lilies,
me throwing walnuts at gas cans
by the barn, stomping mud puddles,
my sticky hands lifting an apple
to my mouth. Here are dogwoods

and hills of corn that lead to more hills
of corn and more corn until the moon
comes up hot and my father
rattles the ice in his gin and tonic,
polishes his guitar. The horses

that dragged the lumber to build
my grandparents' house still stomp
in the back pasture, swirl their tails
at fat, biting flies, and the sizzle of bacon
keeps waking me from my childhood
dreams: cattails snapping
their fingers, a badger's green stare
caught in headlights, my grandfather's
riding mower humming on the lawn,
confetti of clipped grass stuck
to his neck. The clouds here are so long

they stretch from the hidden parts of your blood
across the Atlantic to some lost place where
every ocean is healthy again, plump with whales,
and your forbears stand on cobblestones
around a barrel fire, licking
salted whitefish off their thumbs.

And here you are this morning, climbing
the wood fence I will always carry splinters from,
lifting your body into the smoke of
our leaf fire, great plumes of it reminding us
we were born to keep moving here, keep
leaving here, keep killing these fields and hills,
twisting them into smoke, then bringing them back.

Kid, these are train tracks,

the train never comes.

You smell it anyway, its blue-coal
body. In August, the fringe sticky

with Queen Anne's lace, you might
walk these tracks inside

gigantic noons. I walked them.
You might smash bottles,

start fires, watch clouds from
your back, breathe clouds through

the red sparks of cigarettes.
Take your first sips of bad

sweet wine, cry in a graveyard at night
with your best friend, a half moon

and grave dirt in your hair.
Have your first bad kiss here, like

swallowing a living fish. If you see
the older kids, run, god

knows why. They will chase you
into the waxy halls

of high school. Unlike me,
you will have all your music

in your hand, the best
movies, a phone that calls

everyone at once. Look up.
The big fires of June stars

are so slow and boring they will
keep you awake for good.

Swim the mucky river.
Wash your hair in clover-smell,

the swish of trees. The crows—
you can't not love it

when they chatter the sun down.
Follow gravel roads

to screaming crickets
and beer, sleep out

on the hood of your
hand-me-down Honda,

wake up with yellow flowers
in your mouth. Walk the streets

on the first night
of fall, every tree swelling

with what I can't say
and see in the lit-up houses

beautiful pictures
of strangers.

of November. It strips off the rest
of the leaves, reminds trees
how to shiver. I think to Earth
it looks like the *first* first rain, the water
of the beginning, swirling down hot
into gassy soup. The bubbling stuff
that imagined trees to begin with, and also
mountains, kangaroos, dolphin cartilage,
stoplights. And you, tearing down
hills on Arnold Street, a blur
of training wheels and streamers. And me
in the '80s, crunching Life cereal on the couch
beside my night-owl mother, blue in the light
of David Letterman's grin.

Try to remember, everything that is solid
is not solid. But slowly, always melting. The road
cracks, wrinkles like a folded map. Huge trees
lie down, throb into pulp inside termites.
And the ground drinks you,
though you grow, a tall drink of water,
going down easy. It swallows me faster
and faster. But don't worry. Look at
our neighbor's roof—those fake gray shingles
are crumbling, growing a thick pelt
of moss. Eventually
we all wake up as forest.

AFTER DINNER

I slide clean glasses into place
like rooks. The TV buzzes
like a pharmacy. A uniformed man
explains the president's plan.
I decide to call my brother.
Something has chewed
our wires again.
There's a war on, suffering.
Can I help with this? I open
my guitar case. My guitar can't
sleep: its one eye never closes.

Curls of Smoke

They look soft,
you said, those curls of smoke
above Philadelphia

we saw out the window
of our plane, leaving
the fires of that city,

the wedding of our good friends,
all of that glad crying and yelling,
that tightness in our chests.

What made the smoke,
I asked you—jet trails, ship exhaust,
some kind of suburb fire,

leaf piles going up, or was it
layers, smoke on top of smoke
from several places?

Then we flew into the smoke,
and you saw, you said,
fields and trees

down through it, their colors
changed by it, and it made you
think of the groomsmen,

somehow, our childhood friends
getting fat, sneaking drinks
while their wives were away,

and the ridiculous fight
the bride and groom had
on the wedding night,

the songs we had wept to
still inside them,
the embarrassing speeches

and dance moves
of their fathers:
they were arguing over condoms,

who had lost them,
they told us the next day,
and laughed at it then.

But the night of the fight each wanted the other
to feel how hard it had been,
enduring the shame and hope

of the ceremony, the lilies, the shoulders
of bridesmaids, the noise of rain
on the outdoor pavilion

so loud the homily got lost in it
and the reverend asked God
if it pleased Him, please hold it back,

the rain, but it didn't please Him,
we guessed, because the roar grew,
and we all laughed or strained

to catch what he was saying,
the words of blessing for these two,
wanting to hear

how we, too, might be blessed,
how we might be courageous
enough to raise our kids,

to love or strain enough to make it
together to death.
When I'm dead, you said,

looking down now at the curls of smoke,
throw me from an airplane, into the fields
and trees. My ashes, I mean.

Alfred, the wind in your world
lopes, snow-drunk.
A lone woman walks in it,
her apron scattering salt

brought from her bright kitchen, its white
joining white the way your canvas
leaks through the tops of clouds,
clumps up where snow clumps, in branches,

on the fence. Her face is itself a clump
of color, featureless beneath her black
umbrella bowing to three bare trees,
the only bending thing here, despite

the white weight. You have made everything
upright but unanchored, houses foundationless,
trees with no roots, fences sliding
in place, even her shoes floating

somehow over the snow-vague ground.
What has she come for, out of the warmth
of her house? Does she walk toward
me, carrying some message?

I have read about your throat cancer,
the shame your father felt
losing his money, your life of penury.
I have come here to your road, your fences, your trees,

to this place where nothing touches the ground.
I have come to watch smoke drift out of houses—
and a woman moves against the cold
with what looks like joy.